MH01153374

EXPLORERS OF THE NEW WORLD

BY
WALTER A. HAZEN

COPYRIGHT © 1994 Mark Twain Media, Inc.

ISBN 978–1–58037–062–2
ISBN 1–58037–062–4

Printing No. CD–1832

Mark Twain Media, Inc., Publishers
Distributed by Carson-Dellosa Publishing Company, Inc.

TABLE OF CONTENTS

INTRODUCTION

Having been a teacher of social studies for many years, I am very much aware of the limitations of history textbooks. So much information must be condensed in so little space that only what writers and publishers consider the most important facts can be included. There is little room left for addressing the everyday lives of historical persons.

Explorers of the New World is an attempt to fill this void. Students are presented with interesting narratives of various explorers with each story followed by a fun-filled and challenging puzzle. Also included in each section are three to four activities that span the curriculum. There are vocabulary exercises designed to increase word usage skills and sequencing activities that test a student's ability to arrange events in chronological order. Some stories are followed by activities to enhance critical thinking skills, while other activities attempt to help the student distinguish fact from fiction. There are numerous research projects, as well as opportunities to write journals and simulated newspaper articles. Many stories are followed by math exercises that prove both challenging and entertaining. Finally, a variety of art activities are presented. Sometimes students are asked to simply draw or paint a picture or create a map depicting the route followed by a certain explorer; at other times, they are asked to complete a diorama or some other art form.

Explorers of the New World is more than a whole language book, however. Each short narrative was written to encompass those competencies expected of students in history classes; namely, the ability to understand what brought on the Age of Exploration, the roles played by the various countries and the men who sailed for them, and how their efforts and deeds changed the world and helped usher in modern times.

Finally, this book should be of use to the teacher in a way other than as a supplement to the textbook. Those teachers who find they are sometimes hard pressed to come up with suitable assignments for substitutes should find the puzzles and activities in *Explorers of the New World* of particular interest and use.

—The Author—

VASCO DA GAMA

Europeans in the fifteenth century began to search for an all-water route to the Far East. This region of the world included India, China, and the East Indies. From these faraway places came such desired goods as spices and silk.

An overland route to the East had been used for years, but it was dangerous and very expensive. The cost of bringing goods across land for thousands of miles made the merchandise virtually unaffordable by the time it reached the market in Europe.

In 1486, Bartholomew Diaz, sailing for Portugal, reached the Cape of Good Hope at the southern tip of Africa. His men refused to go farther, however, and he was forced to turn around and sail home.

Eleven years later, King Manuel I sent Vasco da Gama on the same mission. He left Lisbon, Portugal, in 1497 with four ships and over 200 men. Three of his four ships were fast-sailing vessels called caravels. One was commanded by Vasco's brother Paolo. They arrived in Calicut, India, in May 1498.

Da Gama's voyage lasted over two years and covered about 2,000 miles. Before his return to Portugal in 1499, his crews had spent more than 300 days on the open water. Only 60 were left alive at the end of the expedition. Many had died from scurvy, a disease caused by the lack of fresh fruits and vegetables.

In spite of the loss of so many men, was Vasco da Gama's journey successful? From a financial standpoint, yes. He returned with spices, jewels, silk, and other goods valued at 60 times the cost of the trip. He helped to make Portugal the richest country in Europe for a short time in the fifteenth century.

Da Gama received many honors from the king. For finding the first all-water route to India, he was named Admiral of the Sea of the Indies. He became quite wealthy. Before his death in 1524, he also served as Viceroy, or governor, of the Portuguese posts in India.

Name _____ Date _____

CHECKING YOUR VOCABULARY

The word box below contains words from the story about Vasco da Gama that you may or may not know. Use them to fill in the sentences below the box. You may use a dictionary if necessary.

caravel	posts	spices
expedition	route	viceroy
mission	scurvy	voyage

1. An _____ was a trip taken for the purpose of exploration.

2. A person who governed a country or province in the name of a ruler was called a

   _____ .

3. _____ is a disease caused by the lack of fresh fruits and vegetables in

   the diet.

4. A word meaning an assignment or errand is _____ .

5. _____ are seasonings used to flavor food.

6. The Portuguese had forts, or trading _____ , in India.

7. A _____ is a kind of sailing ship.

8. A journey by water is a _____ .

9. A _____ is a way or course traveled in going from one place to another.

EXPOSITORY WRITING ASSIGNMENT

On your own paper write an essay comparing and contrasting today's explorations of space with the voyages of exploration that took place in the fifteenth and sixteenth centuries. Point out similarities as well as differences.

Name _____ Date _____

AN ART ACTIVITY

Make a drawing of a caravel. Label the following:

      1. forecastle   2. bow   3. stern   4. lateen sails

Name_____ Date _____

VASCO DA GAMA CROSSWORD PUZZLE

Use the clues below and information from the narrative to complete the puzzle.

ACROSS

5. Capital of Portugal.
6. City in India where da Gama arrived.
10. Region including India, China, and the East Indies (two words).
11. The Cape of _____ _____ .
13. Cinnamon and ginger are examples.
17. A kind of ship.
19. Da Gama's rank.
20. Disease caused by the lack of fresh fruits and vegetables.

DOWN

1. He sailed to the tip of Africa.
2. A journey by ship.
3. Vasco da Gama's brother.
4. Diaz sailed to the _____ of Africa.
7. They powered da Gama's ships.
8. King of Portugal's name.
9. Da Gama sailed for the king of _____ .
12. Portugal established trading _____ .
14. Country where da Gama sailed to.
15. Goods carried by ships.
16. Da Gama had over 200 _____ .
18. Da Gama became _____ of India.

VASCO DA GAMA
ANSWER KEYS

CHECKING YOUR VOCABULARY (page 3)

1. expedition
2. viceroy
3. scurvy
4. mission
5. spices
6. posts
7. caravel
8. voyage
9. route

CROSSWORD PUZZLE (page 5)

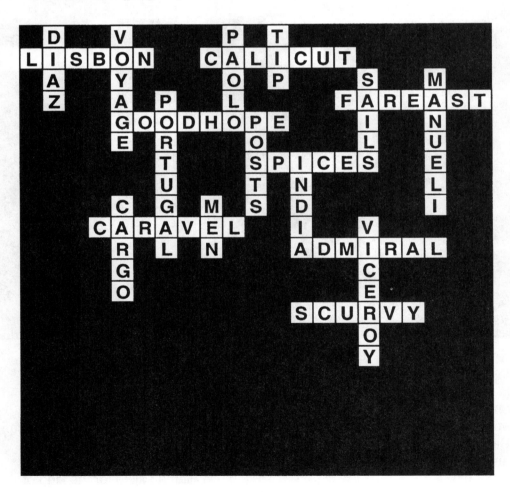

CHRISTOPHER COLUMBUS

You have learned that the Portuguese reached India in 1498. Before that time, other people believed the Far East could be reached by sailing west across the "Ocean Sea," or the Atlantic Ocean, as we know it. One such person was Christopher Columbus.

Columbus was born in Genoa, Italy. As a boy he worked for his father, a weaver. But young Christopher's thoughts were elsewhere. He dreamed of sailing the seas and having adventures in faraway lands. At age 14 he realized his dreams and went to sea. For the remainder of his life he would be a sailor.

Columbus believed that by sailing west he could reach India and other lands rich in jewels, spices, and silk. He thought that Cipango (Japan) and Cathay (China) were less than 3,000 miles away. For years he tried to interest some European country in financing an expedition, or journey.

Finally, King Ferdinand and Queen Isabella of Spain agreed to give Columbus three ships. These were the *Niña*, the *Pinta*, and the *Santa Maria*. On August 3, 1492, he left Palos, Spain, with 88 men. They stopped briefly at the Canary Islands off Africa. Here they made necessary repairs and took on supplies. Columbus then sailed due west out across the Atlantic. He believed that with good weather he would reach Cipango in one month.

But Columbus misjudged the size of the earth. He did not know that North, Central, and South America lay between Europe and Asia. He had no way of knowing that Japan was more than 10,000 miles away.

After two months at sea, Columbus's crew was ready to mutiny. They were restless and afraid. They told him on October 9 that if land was not seen in several days they would force him to turn back. Luckily for Columbus, land was spotted on October 12.

Columbus had landed at an island that is now part of the Bahamas. He thought the island was Cipango. He named it San Salvador and claimed it for Spain. He sailed farther and discovered Jamaica, Puerto Rico, Hispaniola, and Cuba. He mistakenly thought Cuba and Haiti (part of Hispaniola) were Cathay.

Columbus returned to Spain after a voyage of 224 days, and for awhile he was a hero. Ferdinand and Isabella sent him back to the New World on three more expeditions. But he never found the gold, spices, and jewels he sought. He quickly fell out of favor with the king and queen. After a third voyage of failure, he was sent back to Spain in chains. Finally, after a fourth unsuccessful expedition from 1502 to 1504, he returned to Spain for the last time.

Columbus by now was a sick and disheartened man, and he died in disgrace in 1506. He never realized that the people he called "Indians" were inhabitants of a New World. He died still believing he had reached the Far East.

Name _____ Date _____

THEN AND NOW

You have learned that Japan was formerly called Cipango and China was once known as Cathay. Below are some former names of various places and countries. Write beside them what they are called today.

Persia _____

Mesopotamia _____

Gaul _____

Rhodesia _____

Siam _____

Ceylon _____

PREPARE A JOURNAL

Through Professor Gray Matter's time machine, you are whisked back to October 1492 aboard Columbus's flagship, the *Santa Maria.*

Compose a journal describing your experience. Be sure to include the following:

1. A description of the *Santa Maria.*

2. Highlights of the journey across the Atlantic.

3. The mood of the crew in the last few days prior to the sighting of land.

4. The crew's reaction upon hearing the cry "Land ho!"

WRITE A LETTER

Pretend you are Christopher Columbus. Using your own paper, write a letter to King Ferdinand and Queen Isabella requesting that they sponsor your expedition to find a shorter sea route to the Indies. Explain your plan and what supplies you will need.

Name_____ Date _____

READING A TIME LINE

The following time line gives you significant dates and events concerning the voyage of Columbus. Use it to answer the questions below.

Left Palos, Spain	Reached Canary Islands	Left Canary Islands	Sailors ready to mutiny	Reached San Salvador	Returned to Spain
August 3, 1492	Aug. 12	Sept. 7	Oct. 10	Oct. 12	March 15, 1493

1. How many days did it take Columbus to reach the Canary Islands? _____

2. How long did Columbus stay in the Canary Islands? _____

3. Columbus left the Canary Islands on September 7 and arrived in America on October

    12. This was a journey of _____ weeks.

4. How many weeks did it take Columbus to sail from Palos, Spain, to San Salvador?

    _____

5. Columbus's voyage began on August 3, 1492, and ended on March 15, 1493, a period

    of _____ weeks.

AN ART ACTIVITY

On a separate sheet of paper, draw and color or paint a picture depicting Columbus's landing in the New World.

Name_____ Date _____

CHRISTOPHER COLUMBUS CROSSWORD PUZZLE
Use the clues below and information from the narrative to complete the puzzle.

ACROSS

3. The occupation of Columbus's father.
4. When sailors overthrow their captain and take over the ship.
5. Islands off the coast of Africa where Columbus stopped for repairs and supplies.
6. Columbus received ships from this country.
12. Old name for Japan.
13. Queen ____ of Spain.
15. Island where Columbus first touched land in America.
17. Fourteen-hundred and ninety- ____ .
18. One of Columbus's ships.
20. What Columbus called the natives of America.
21. Country that is part of Hispaniola.

DOWN

1. What the Atlantic Ocean used to be called.
2. Columbus thought by sailing ____ he could reach the East.
5. Island of the West Indies discovered by Columbus.
6. One of Columbus's ships (two words).
7. Columbus discovered a ____ World.
8. Puerto ____ .
9. Group of islands where Columbus landed in the New World.
10. Port Columbus sailed from in August 1492.
11. King ____ of Spain.
14. Old name for China.
16. Columbus's birthplace.
17. Columbus made four ____ to America.
19. One of Columbus's ships.

CHRISTOPHER COLUMBUS
ANSWER KEYS

THEN AND NOW (page 8)
1. Persia: Iran
2. Mesopotamia: Iraq
3. Gaul: France
4. Rhodesia: Zimbabwe
5. Siam: Thailand
6. Ceylon: Sri Lanka

READING A TIME LINE (page 9)
1. 9 days
2. 26 days
3. 5 weeks
4. 10 weeks
5. 32 weeks

CROSSWORD PUZZLE (page 10)

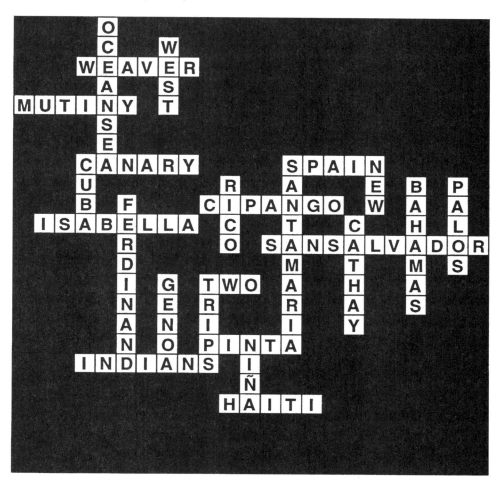

JOHN CABOT

Five years after Columbus came to America, an Italian living in England had a similar dream. He asked King Henry VII to finance an expedition to find the Northwest Passage. You will remember that Europeans thought there was a waterway through North America directly to the Far East. We know today that such a waterway does exist, but it is far too winding and difficult to be practical.

The person of whom we speak was Giovanni Caboto, an Italian living in Bristol, England. Caboto was born in Genoa, Italy, and had been a merchant in Venice. He moved to England in 1490 and became a wealthy merchant there. Afterwards, he was known as John Cabot. The name John Cabot is the English version of Giovanni Caboto.

King Henry agreed to give Cabot a small ship called the *Matthew*. Its crew of 18 included Cabot's son, Sebastian. The king also gave Cabot a charter to claim any new land he found for the English crown.

Cabot left Bristol, England, on May 2, 1497. He followed a route much farther north than Columbus had five years before. After six weeks at sea, the *Matthew* touched land somewhere off present-day Canada. Cabot had probably reached either Nova Scotia or Newfoundland. He explored this northernmost coast of America, taking it to be China, the land of the Great Khan.

John Cabot returned to England, thinking he had found the northeast coast of Asia. Henry VII was impressed and financed a second expedition. This time Cabot had a fleet of five ships and a crew of 300. Setting sail in May 1498, he crossed the Atlantic and this time explored all the way from Greenland in the north to North Carolina in the south. But, like all the others, he never found the Northwest Passage.

A disappointed John Cabot found no gold or spices, but he did discover the rich cod-fishing grounds off Newfoundland. Much wealth would later pour into England because of this discovery.

The end of Cabot's second voyage is shrouded in mystery. Historians disagree as to what happened to him. Some maintain that he returned to England and disappeared from history. The more widely accepted belief, however, is that he went down with his ship in a storm off the coast of Newfoundland.

The voyages of John Cabot were important because they gave England claim to the mainland of North America. This claim paved the way for the founding of the English colonies in the early seventeenth century.

Name _____ Date _____

THE NAME'S THE SAME

You have learned that John in Italian is Giovanni. John appears in other languages as Jean, Juan, Johann, and Ivan, among others.

Below are some famous people with the name John. Look them up in an encyclopedia. Write the name of the country they are from and tell why they are famous.

1. Jean Ribault   Country: _____

Why famous: _____

2. Johann Gutenberg   Country: _____

Why famous: _____

3. Juan Ponce de Leon   Country: _____

Why famous: _____

4. Ivan Turgenev   Country: _____

Why famous: _____

5. Ignace (Jan) Paderewski   Country: _____

Why famous: _____

6. Johann Sebastian Bach   Country: _____

Why famous: _____

7. Giovanni Giolitti   Country: _____

Why famous: _____

8. Ivan the Terrible   Country: _____

Why famous: _____

Name _____ Date _____

UNDERSTANDING THE MAIN FACTS

Write short answers for the following questions:

1. What was John Cabot's occupation?

_____

2. Where did Cabot first touch land in America?

_____

3. Why did Henry VII finance Cabot's second expedition?

_____

_____

4. What seems to have happened to Cabot?

_____

_____

5. What discovery of Cabot's was financially beneficial to England?

_____

6. Why were the voyages of Cabot important?

_____

_____

MAKE A COMPARISON

Compare the first voyages of Cabot and Columbus with regard to:

   a. routes taken

   b. time required to cross the Atlantic

   c. where they landed in the New World

   d. significance of their expeditions

Name _____ Date _____

JOHN CABOT CROSSWORD PUZZLE

Use the clues below and information from the narrative to complete the puzzle.

ACROSS

3. Cabot might have landed here on his first voyage (two words).
5. Cabot found these fish off Newfoundland.
8. On his first voyage, Cabot had a _____ of 18.
9. Route to Asia Cabot was sent to find.
14. Cabot had been a merchant here.
16. Cabot thought he had reached this continent.
17. On his second voyage, Cabot had _____ ships.
18. Cabot's birthplace.
19. Cabot's son.
20. Cabot's ship.

DOWN

1. Cabot sailed as far south as this state (two words).
2. Cabot's real last name.
4. Where Cabot's ship went down.
6. Cabot sailed from here.
7. Chinese ruler, the Great _____ .
10. Cabot had this many ships on his first voyage.
11. Cabot set _____ on May 2, 1497.
12. Cabot's real first name.
13. The _____ World.
15. Cabot's expedition led to the founding of the English _____ .

JOHN CABOT
ANSWER KEYS

THE NAME'S THE SAME (page 13)

1. Jean Ribault: Country: France.
   Why famous: Helped establish a French colony in the New World.

2. Johann Gutenberg: Country: Germany.
   Why famous: Invented the printing press with movable type.

3. Juan Ponce de Leon: Country: Spain.
   Why famous: Explorer who discovered Florida.

4. Ivan Turgenev: Country: Russia.
   Why famous: Famous novelist.

5. Ignace (Jan) Paderewski:
   Country: Poland.
   Why famous: Great pianist, composer, and statesman.

6. Johann Sebastian Bach:
   Country: Germany.
   Why famous: Composer and organist of the Baroque period.

7. Giovanni Giolitti: Country: Italy.
   Why famous: Statesman; Prime Minister of Italy.

8. Ivan the Terrible: Country: Russia.
   Why famous: Czar of Russia; brutal; killed his own son.

UNDERSTANDING THE MAIN FACTS (page 14)

1. merchant
2. at either Nova Scotia or Newfoundland
3. he thought Cabot had reached China
4. he was lost in a storm at sea
5. the cod-fishing grounds off Newfoundland

6. they gave England claim to land in North America

MAKE A COMPARISON (page 14)

a. routes taken:
   Cabot left England and took a northern route to Canada; Columbus sailed from Spain, a more southerly route that took him to the West Indies.

b. time required to cross the Atlantic:
   Columbus: 5 weeks after leaving the Canary Islands; Cabot: 6 weeks.

c. where they landed in the New World:
   Cabot landed at either Nova Scotia or Newfoundland; Columbus at San Salvador Island in the West Indies.

d. significance of their expeditions:
   Columbus discovered a New World; Cabot's voyages gave England claim to land in North America.

CROSSWORD PUZZLE (page 15)

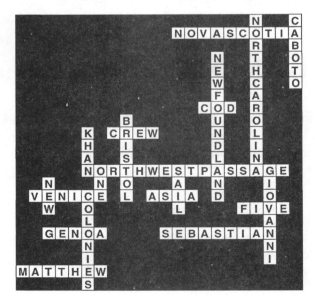

VASCO NUÑEZ DE BALBOA

You may have learned that Francisco Pizarro conquered the Incas in 1531. This feat, however, might have been accomplished by another conquistador had he not been the victim of misfortune and circumstance.

Vasco Nuñez de Balboa was born in 1475 in Jerez de Los Caballeros, Spain. Little is known of his early life. He came to the New World in 1500 hoping to make his fortune. Finding no gold, he tried his hand unsuccessfully at farming in Hispaniola. Hispaniola is a large island in the West Indies that is today divided between the nations of Haiti and the Dominican Republic.

Balboa borrowed a sizable amount of money and fell heavily in debt. To avoid paying back his loans, he stowed away on a ship bound for Panama. Panama is an isthmus, or narrow strip of land, that connects North and South America and is bordered by the Atlantic and Pacific Oceans. Today the Panama Canal provides a passage between these great bodies of water.

Balboa took control of the expedition that landed in Panama in 1509. There he established the colony of Darien and became its governor. He made friends with the Indians and even married a chief's daughter. From the Indians, Balboa heard two very exciting tales: one of a great sea that lay beyond the mountains of Panama, and the other of Indians to the south who dined from golden plates and cups. These Indians, of course, were the Incas.

With 190 soldiers (including Francisco Pizarro) and 1,000 Indians, Balboa set out to cross the jungles and mountains of Panama. On September 25, 1513, Balboa first saw the Pacific Ocean from high atop a mountain. He was the first European to see the eastern shore of this magnificent "sea." Several days later, in full armor and with sword and flag in hand, he waded into the water and claimed it for Spain. He called his discovery the South Sea. Another famous explorer, Ferdinand Magellan, would later name it the Pacific Ocean.

Balboa never had a chance to follow up on the second tale he had heard from the Indians: that of a great Indian empire to the south. In 1517, King Ferdinand of Spain sent Pedro Arias de Avila to become governor of Panama. Avila soon became jealous of Balboa, who was very popular because of his expeditions. The new governor put Balboa in jail and had him tried for treason. After a short time, he and four friends were beheaded.

Spain had hoped that the great "sea" discovered by Balboa would turn out to be the long-sought route to Cathay, or China. But it only proved that Asia was even farther away than anyone had previously thought.

Name _____ Date _____

A GEOGRAPHY EXERCISE

Hispaniola is about 400 miles long and 150 miles wide. Compare its size with these other islands of the West Indies. Give the length and width for each island.

1. Cuba _____

2. Puerto Rico _____

3. Jamaica _____

4. Watling Island (San Salvador) _____

FOR RESEARCH

Prepare a report of two to three pages in length on the history of one of the following:

1. Haiti

2. The Dominican Republic

3. The Panama Canal

ART ACTIVITIES

Choose one of the following art forms and depict Balboa's discovery of the Pacific Ocean:

a. diorama

b. mural

c. comic strip

d. clay models

Name _____ Date _____

DRAW A MAP

Draw a map of the island of Hispaniola. Write in the names of Haiti and the Dominican Republic, the two nations that share the island. Be sure to include the capitals of each.

Name _____ Date _____

VASCO NUÑEZ DE BALBOA CROSSWORD PUZZLE
Use the clues below and information from the narrative to complete the puzzle.

ACROSS

2. Narrow strip of land connecting two larger landmasses.
4. An Incan might drink from a golden _____ .
5. What Balboa discovered (two words).
8. Crime Balboa was accused of.
11. Pedro Arias de _____ .
13. China's continent.
17. _____ Republic, part of Hispaniola.
19. What Balboa did unsuccessfully in Hispaniola.

DOWN

1. Balboa fell heavily in _____ .
2. An Indian of Peru.
3. Balboa called the Pacific the South _____ .
4. The Panama _____ .
6. Old name for China.
7. King _____ of Spain.
9. What Balboa hoped to become in the New World.
10. Balboa's native country.
12. Balboa's first name.
14. Part of Hispaniola.
15. Avila beheaded this many.
16. Colony Balboa established.
18. Jerez de Los _____ .

VASCO NUÑEZ DE BALBOA
ANSWER KEYS

A GEOGRAPHY EXERCISE (page 18)
1. Cuba: length 759 miles; width 135 miles
2. Puerto Rico: length 100 miles; width 35 miles
3. Jamaica: length 148 miles; width 52 miles
4. Watling Island (San Salvador): 60 square miles; approximately 10 miles long, 6 miles wide

DRAW A MAP (page 19)
     Maps should include the names of the two countries, Haiti and the Dominican Republic, plus their capitals, Port-au-Prince and Santo Domingo.

CROSSWORD PUZZLE (page 20)

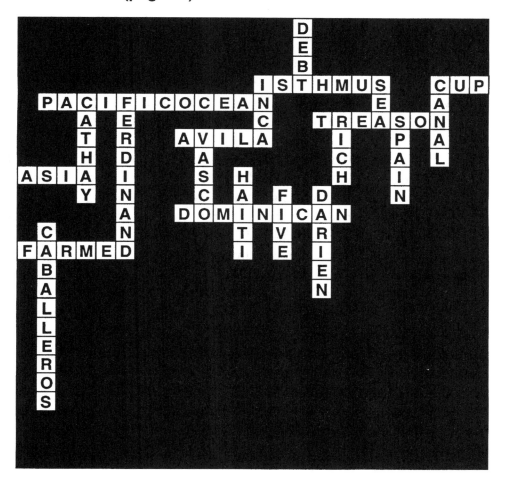

HERNANDO CORTÉS

Hernando Cortés is probably the most famous of the Spanish conquistadors, or conquerors. He is remembered for destroying the Aztec Empire and conquering Mexico for Spain. Though a brilliant military leader, he was cruel and brutal toward the Indians.

As a young man, Cortés studied to become a lawyer. But, like Columbus, he dreamed of adventure. In 1504, he came to Hispaniola in the New World as a farmer. Seven years later he took part in the conquest of Cuba. In 1519, he was sent by the governor of Cuba to conquer Mexico.

Cortés founded the city of Veracruz in Mexico and then marched on and destroyed the Aztec holy city of Cholula. With 500 soldiers and 16 horses, he then proceeded on to Tenochtitlan, the Aztec capital. Tenochtitlan is today called Mexico City.

Tenochtitlan was an unusual city. It was built on an island in the middle of a lake. Access to the city was over a causeway, a raised road that crossed a wetland. Such terrain was easily defended by the Aztecs, who killed many of Cortés's men before they were defeated.

Several factors proved to be in the Spaniards' favor. The Aztecs believed that Cortés was Quetzelcoatl, a god who was supposed to return one day as a bearded white man. Because of this, Montezuma, the Aztec emperor, welcomed Cortés warmly. The Aztecs also believed that each Spanish soldier and his horse was one being. They had never seen horses before and were naturally terrified of them. They assumed that man and horse together was some kind of magical animal. Imagine their surprise when a conquistador dismounted and walked away!

The Spaniards were further aided by the hatred that other Indians of Mexico felt toward the Aztecs. This was because an important feature of Aztec religion was human sacrifice. Most of the victims for this practice came from prisoners taken by the Aztecs in war. Little wonder that many of these Indians were more than ready to help Cortés in his conquest of Mexico.

Because of Hernando Cortés and later Spanish explorers, Spain became the leading power of Europe. The gold and silver taken from the Indians of the Americas also made Spain the wealthiest nation in Europe.

Cortés later turned northward for further adventure. In 1536 he founded the first European settlement in Lower California. As a closing note, lovers of such treats as chocolate candy and ice cream owe a debt of gratitude to this famous explorer. He introduced chocolate to Spain in the early sixteenth century.

Name _____ Date _____

ARRANGE IN CHRONOLOGICAL ORDER

Using the numbers 1 through 5, arrange in order the following events concerning Hernando Cortés.

_____ Cortés establishes the first European settlement in Lower California.

_____ Cortés comes to Hispaniola as a farmer.

_____ Cortés lands in Mexico.

_____ Cortés destroys the holy city of Cholula.

_____ Cortés takes part in the conquest of Cuba.

INTERVIEWING

Pretend that you are Diego Gonzalez, a reporter for the *Barcelona Blah*, who has accompanied Cortés on his expedition to Mexico. Write a report on your interview with an Aztec Indian who has just seen a horse for the first time.

ART ACTIVITIES

1. Draw and color or paint a picture depicting the clothing and weapons of the typical Spanish conquistador.

2. Research ancient Aztec artwork, crafts, and clothing with the help of an encyclopedia or a book on ancient Indian civilizations. Draw and color an example of an Aztec artifact.

Name _____ Date _____

CHOOSE THE APPROPRIATE MEANING

As you know, many words have more than one meaning. With each word listed below, underline the meaning that best describes the word as it is used in our narrative of Cortés.

1. sacrifice: giving up of one thing for another

    an offering to a god

    a bunt in baseball that advances a runner

2. power: energy that can do work

    authority or influence

    a strong nation

3. settlement: colony

    payment

    arrangement

4. practice: business of a doctor or lawyer

    habit, ritual, or custom

    do something regularly in order to gain skill

5. found: start or establish

    past tense of find

    to cast from molten metal

6. introduce: make known by name to someone else

    bring in for the first time

    to insert

7. factor: a cause that helps bring about a result

    a number that, when multiplied by another number, forms a product

    a person who acts as an agent for someone else

Name _____ Date _____

HERNANDO CORTÉS CROSSWORD PUZZLE

Use the clues below and information from the narrative to complete the puzzle.

ACROSS

1. Spanish word for conqueror.
3. The governor of _____ sent Cortés to conquer Mexico.
6. Aztec emperor.
7. Aztec god.
9. Cortés conquered the _____ Empire.
12. The Aztecs thought a soldier and his _____ were one being.
13. Where Spain is.
16. Aztec holy city.
18. City founded by Cortés in Mexico.
19. Religious practice of the Aztecs (two words).

DOWN

2. Aztec capital city.
3. A road over a wetland.
4. Profession Cortés studied for.
5. At first, the Aztecs thought Cortés was a _____ .
8. Tenochtitlan was built in the middle of a _____ .
10. Part of the New World conquered by Cortés.
11. Valuable metal Spain got from Mexico.
14. Tasty treat introduced into Europe by Cortés.
15. Cortés founded the first European settlement in Lower _____ .
17. What Tenochtitlan is called today (two words).

HERNANDO CORTÉS
ANSWER KEYS

ARRANGE IN CHRONOLOGICAL ORDER (page 22)
5, 1, 3, 4, 2

CHOOSE THE APPROPRIATE MEANING (page 23)
1. sacrifice: an offering to a god.
2. power: a strong nation.
3. settlement: colony.
4. practice: habit, ritual, or custom.
5. found: start or establish.
6. introduce: bring in for the first time.
7. factor: a cause that helps bring about a result.

CROSSWORD PUZZLE (page 24)

FERDINAND MAGELLAN

Ferdinand Magellan was a Portuguese sea captain who sailed in the service of Spain. Although he did not live to see its completion, he is credited with leading the first expedition to sail around the world.

Magellan was born in 1480 in Sabrosa, Portugal, the son of a nobleman. As a boy he served as a page to the Portuguese queen. He joined the army as a young man and spent seven years as a soldier in India and the East Indies. There he saw firsthand the wealth of that rich land.

At this time in history, Portugal controlled the eastern route to the East. The Portuguese king had no interest in finding a western course. Remember, Columbus and others had searched for this route but failed in their efforts. In 1517, Magellan went to Spain and proposed to King Charles V a plan to find this western route. Magellan's wish was granted. On September 20, 1519, he sailed from Seville, Spain, with five ships and 270 men. His destination was the coast of South America. His plan was to sail down this coast and hopefully find an opening through which to sail on to the East Indies.

Magellan reached the area of present-day Argentina on December 11, 1519. There he had to put down a revolt of some of his officers, who resented being under the command of a Portuguese. He restored his authority by having several put to death and one marooned, or left, on the deserted coast.

Sailing down the coast of South America, Magellan discovered at the tip the strait that today bears his name. For 38 days and 350 miles his ships wound their way through the narrow opening. Finally, on November 28, 1520, he entered the South Sea. He renamed the ocean Pacific, meaning "peaceful," because on that day the waters were unusually calm.

Magellan was down to three ships. One had been wrecked and another had secretly returned to Spain. He sailed on. For 98 days no land was sighted. He and his men were reduced to eating leather, sawdust, and rats. Many starved to death. Others had scurvy.

After three months, the expedition reached the Mariana Islands where they rested and took on supplies. Two months later, they reached the Philippines. It was here that Magellan foolishly participated in a native quarrel and was killed. Two more ships were lost, along with 24 more men. The one remaining ship, the *Victory*, escaped. It sailed on to the Molucca Islands in the East Indies and loaded up with spices. Under the command of Juan Sebastian del Cano, the *Victory* returned to Seville in September 1522. The complete voyage had taken 36 months.

Magellan's expedition was important because it proved that the world was round and that it was possible to sail around it. The trip also gave mapmakers a true indication of the size of the world.

Name _____ Date _____

THEN AND NOW

Magellan's expedition took three years to journey around the world. Travel today, of course, is much faster. Consult an encyclopedia or a book on transportation and travel to find out how long it takes each of the following to accomplish what Magellan did:

1. The space shuttle   _____ hours

2. A jet airliner   _____ hours

3. A cruise ship   _____ days

TWO MATH ACTIVITIES

1. It took Magellan's ships 38 days to travel the 350 miles through the strait that bears his

name. This was an average of _____ miles per day. (Round off your answer.)

2. Magellan left Seville, Spain, on September 20, 1519. He reached the coast of Argentina

on December 11, 1519. How many days did it take him to complete the trip? _____

SEQUENCING

Put the following events in order by writing the numbers 1 to 5 on the lines to the left.

_____ Magellan entered the Pacific Ocean.

_____ Magellan reached Argentina.

_____ Magellan left Spain to begin his voyage.

_____ Del Cano completed the voyage around the world.

_____ Magellan is killed in the Philippines.

Name_____ Date _____

UNDERSTANDING WHAT YOU HAVE READ

Write short answers to the following questions:

1. Why did some of Magellan's officers rebel against his authority?

_____

_____

2. Why did Magellan call the large ocean he entered the "Pacific"?

_____

_____

3. What led to Magellan's death in the Philippines?

_____

_____

4. What man completed Magellan's expedition?

_____

5. List two reasons why Magellan's expedition was important.

_____

_____

_____

Name_____ Date _____

FERDINAND MAGELLAN CROSSWORD PUZZLE

Use the clues below and information from the narrative to complete the puzzle.

ACROSS

1. Where Magellan was killed.
6. Islands where Magellan took on supplies.
9. Magellan's expedition proved the world was _____ .
11. A journey by ship.
13. Magellan led the first expedition to _____ around the world.
14. The _____ Indies.
16. What the *Victory* managed to do.
18. Juan Sebastian del _____ .
21. Port from which Magellan sailed on September 20, 1519.

DOWN

2. ____ World.
3. Magellan's birthplace (two words).
4. Ferdinand _____ .
5. What Magellan had to eat to keep from starving.
7. Where Magellan landed on December 11, 1519.
8. Country Magellan sailed for.
10. Magellan's dad's rank.
12. Magellan was one as a boy.
15. The Strait of Magellan is at the _____ of South America.
17. The *Victory* loaded up with _____ in the Molucca Islands.
19. What Pacific means.
20. Only ship to return from Magellan's expedition.

FERDINAND MAGELLAN
ANSWER KEYS

THEN AND NOW (page 28)
1. Approximately 1 to $1\frac{1}{2}$ hours.
2. Approximately 36 hours.
3. Approximately 35–40 days.

TWO MATH ACTIVITIES (page 28)
1. 9
2. 82

SEQUENCING (page 28)
3, 2, 1, 5, 4

UNDERSTANDING WHAT YOU HAVE READ (page 29)
1. Being Spanish, they resented being under the command of a Portuguese.
2. The waters were unusually calm on the day he entered the ocean.
3. He took part in a quarrel between the natives.
4. Juan Sebastian del Cano.
5. It proved that the world was round; mapmakers had a better idea of the real size of the world.

CROSSWORD PUZZLE (page 30)

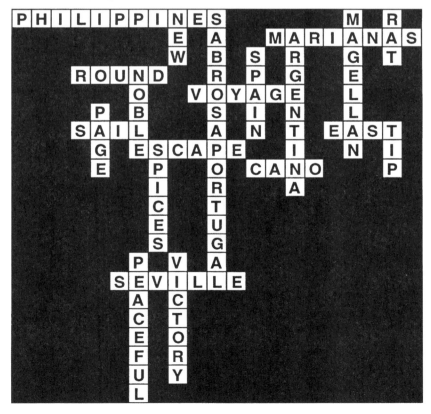

FRANCISCO PIZARRO

Shortly after Hernando Cortés conquered the Aztecs of Mexico, another Spanish conquistador did the same to the Incas of Peru. His name was Francisco Pizarro. History tells us that he was just as cruel as Cortés.

When Francisco Pizarro was born, his mother was so poor that she left him at the door of a church. Because he had no real family, Francisco never learned to read and write. As a boy he worked as a swineherd, taking care of pigs.

When Pizarro was old enough, he became a soldier. He came to the New World in 1510 seeking fame and fortune. In 1513, he accompanied Vasco de Balboa in his discovery of the Pacific Ocean. Afterwards, Pizarro became a cattle rancher in Panama.

In the 1520s, Pizarro and some friends made two trips to Peru. What they saw was unbelievable: gold was everywhere, even lining the outer walls of temples. Returning to Spain with samples of gold ornaments, Pizarro convinced the king to finance an expedition to Peru.

Pizarro, along with his four brothers, landed in Peru in 1531. He had 180 men and 27 horses. With this small army he was able to conquer an empire of some six million Incas. This was due largely to the Incas being involved in a civil war. They were in no position to defend their empire against the Spaniards.

Pizarro captured Cuzco, the Incan capital. He took Atahualpa, the Incan emperor, prisoner and held him for ransom. Pizarro informed the Indians that Atahualpa would be freed if they filled a room with gold and jewels. The Incas readily obeyed. Gold meant nothing to them except as a means of decorating, so they quickly filled the room with the valuable metal. Then they waited for Atahualpa to be released.

But Pizarro proved to be just as untrustworthy as Cortés. Instead of freeing the Incan emperor, he had him strangled to death. All of Atahualpa's chief nobles and officials were killed also. With no one to lead them, the Incas of Peru were easily subdued by the Spaniards.

After the murder of Atahualpa, Pizarro had all of the gold melted into ingots, or bars. The total value of this treasure was more than nine million dollars. Pizarro sent one-fifth of this wealth to the king in Spain and divided the rest among his soldiers. He then founded the city of Lima, which became the new capital of Peru. Here he ruled with the title of marquis until 1541. In that year he was assassinated.

Pizarro's death was associated with the division of the Incan gold. One of the leaders of the expedition, Diego de Almagro, was not satisfied with the way the spoils were divided. As a result, Pizarro's brother Hernando had Almagro beheaded. Almagro's son later avenged his father's death. He killed Pizarro in his palace in Lima in 1541.

Francisco Pizarro added the lands of the Incas to the Spanish Empire. The treasury of Spain continued to bulge with the gold and silver of the New World.

Name_____ Date _____

FACT OR OPINION

The following statements refer to Francisco Pizarro, the Spaniards, and the Inca Indians. On the line to the left of each sentence, write "F" if you think it is a fact or "O" if you consider it an opinion.

_____ 1. The Spaniards were intellectually superior to the Indians.

_____ 2. Pizarro enjoyed his years as a rancher in Panama.

_____ 3. The Spaniards murdered Atahualpa, the Incan emperor.

_____ 4. Pizarro was more cruel than Cortés.

_____ 5. The Spaniards were militarily superior to the Indians.

_____ 6. Except for decoration, gold held no special value to the Incas.

_____ 7. Pizarro proved to be untrustworthy in his dealing with the Incas.

_____ 8. The gold Pizarro took from the Indians made him a happy man.

A MATH ACTIVITY

The value of the gold taken from the Incas was estimated at nine million dollars. If Pizarro sent one-fifth of this to the Spanish king, how much did he keep for himself and his men? $ _____

FOR FURTHER RESEARCH

Prepare a two-page report on one of the following topics:

1. How Gold Is Mined.

2. Machu Picchu (an Incan city high in the Andes).

3. Everyday Life of the Inca Indians.

Name _____ Date _____

MAKE A SHOEBOX DIORAMA

Make a shoebox diorama depicting one of the following scenes from the life of the Incas:

1. A farmer working in his fields.
2. A craftsman making ornaments of gold.
3. Daily activities in an Incan home.

AN ART ACTIVITY

In the space provided or on your own paper, draw and color an example of ancient Incan art, sculpture, or craftsmanship. You can find these in an encyclopedia or in a book on ancient Indian civilizations.

Name_____ Date _____

FRANCISCO PIZARRO CROSSWORD PUZZLE

Use the clues below and information from the narrative to complete the puzzle.

ACROSS

1. Pizarro sought _____ and fortune.
3. Building in which Pizarro was killed.
6. He was beheaded by Hernando Pizarro.
7. Pizarro's job as a young man.
11. Peru, _____ of the Incas.
12. _____ Pizarro.
13. Pizarro's gold ingots were worth nine _____ dollars.
14. Peruvian capital built by Pizarro.
17. Incan capital.
18. Country conquered by Pizarro.

DOWN

2. Incan emperor.
3. Pizarro's mother was very _____ .
4. Where Pizarro was a cattle rancher.
5. Number of brothers Pizarro had.
7. Pizarro's native country.
8. One of Pizarro's brothers.
9. Indian empire conquered by Pizarro.
10. Discoverer of the Pacific Ocean.
13. Pizarro's title as ruler of Peru.
15. Gold bar.
16. Pizarro could not _____ or write.

FRANCISCO PIZARRO
ANSWER KEYS

FACT OR OPINION? (page 33)
1. O
2. O
3. F
4. O
5. F
6. F
7. F
8. O

A MATH ACTIVITY (page 33)
$7,200,000

CROSSWORD PUZZLE (page 35)

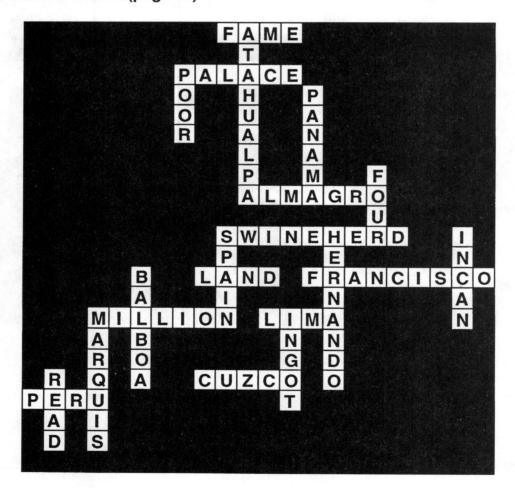

JACQUES CARTIER

The French entered the Age of Exploration in the early sixteenth century. Like the other nations of Europe, France was interested in finding an all-water route to the East. In 1534, King Francis I sent Jacques Cartier to the New World. His mission was to find the Northwest Passage. The Northwest Passage was widely believed to be a water route through Canada to China. It did not exist, but the countries of Europe spent much time, money, and energy trying to find it.

Jacques Cartier was born in St. Malo, France. He became an expert sailor and navigator. On May 6, 1534, he sailed for North America with three ships and 61 men. Landing in Newfoundland, his men made a 30-foot cross of wood and planted it in the sand. Cartier thus claimed Canada for France.

Cartier made a second trip to Canada in 1535. This time he discovered the St. Lawrence River. Thinking that this mighty river led to Indian civilizations as rich as those in Mexico and Peru, he sailed up it as far as the Indian village of Hochelaga. (Hochelaga would later become the city of Montreal.) Here he found the Iroquois Indians to be friendly and courteous. The French offered to share their hardtack and red wine with their new friends. The Indians refused, thinking the French were eating wood and drinking blood!

The winter of 1535 had set in, and Cartier was unable to return to France. He and his men were forced to stay the winter with the Iroquois at Hochelaga. Because they lacked fresh fruits and vegetables, many of the Frenchmen died of scurvy. It is interesting to note that those who accepted and drank the Indian cure for scurvy recovered. The Iroquois had learned to make a brew from the branches of the hemlock tree that apparently cured this disease.

Cartier returned to France with samples of what he thought was gold. What he really had carried back was "false gold." This was probably either copper or iron pyrite. Pyrite is a combination of iron and sulfur that has a yellowish color.

King Francis I sent Cartier back to Canada for a third time in 1541. This time he was to set up a permanent French settlement. He succeeded, but the colony lasted only a year.

Cartier never found any gold in New France, as the French Empire came to be called. Nor did he find the Northwest Passage. For his efforts, however, Francis I made him an admiral in the French navy.

Why were Cartier's explorations important? A look at a map will give you the answer. The St. Lawrence River proved to be the gateway to the continent. It led to the Great Lakes and to the interior of North America. From here the French would fan out and establish the fur trade that brought great wealth to their country.

Name _____ Date _____

BONUS MATH PROBLEMS

The ships of Cartier and other explorers moved very slowly, and their knot speed was low compared to modern ships.

The speed of ships is measured in knots instead of miles. A knot is equivalent to 6,080 feet traveled in one hour. Remembering that there are 5,280 feet in a mile, convert the following knots to miles per hour (MPH).

1. 22 knots = _____ MPH

2. 30 knots = _____ MPH

3. 18 knots = _____ MPH

A ship traveling at 20 knots would journey 121,600 feet in one hour, or 28 miles. In 24 hours, the ship would travel _____ miles.

DRAW A MAP

Draw a map of the part of North America that made up New France. Be sure to include the following on your map:

1. The Mississippi, Ohio, and St. Lawrence Rivers.

2. The Great Lakes.

3. New Orleans, Montreal, and Quebec.

Name_____ Date _____

INTERPRETING A LINE GRAPH

The line graph below shows the approximate number of days required to cross the Atlantic by various ships throughout history.

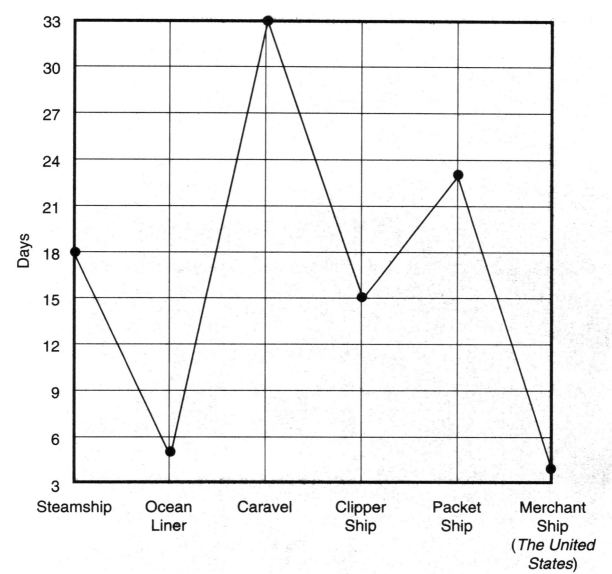

Use the graph to answer these questions:

1. Which ship made the fastest time? _____

2. Which ship took the longest number of days to cross the Atlantic?_____

3. Which ship covered the journey in 15 days?_____

4. How many more days did a steamship require than an ocean liner?_____

Name _____ Date _____

JACQUES CARTIER CROSSWORD PUZZLE

Use the clues below and information from the narrative to complete the puzzle.

ACROSS

3. Jacques _____ .
5. The St. Lawrence leads to these (two words).
9. Number of trips to the New World made by Cartier.
10. Where the Northwest Passage was supposed to lead to.
12. St. _____, Cartier's birthplace.
13. Cartier landed here in 1534.
14. Month when Cartier set sail on his first voyage.
16. Disease caused by the lack of fresh fruits and vegetables.
18. What Montreal is.
19. Northwest _____ .

DOWN

1. Iroquois village.
2. What the French drank.
4. King _____ of France.
6. Cartier made his _____ trip to Canada in 1541.
7. Naval rank given to Cartier.
8. River discovered by Cartier.
11. Cartier's settlement lasted one _____ .
15. North _____ Passage.
17. Cartier claimed this land for France.
20. Cartier found false _____ .

JACQUES CARTIER
ANSWER KEYS

BONUS MATH PROBLEMS (page 38)

1. 22 knots = 25.3 MPH
2. 30 knots = 34.5 MPH
3. 18 knots = 20.7 MPH

(Note: a nautical mile is equal to approximately 1.15 statute or land miles. The knots listed to the left are multiplied by 1.15 to arrive at the MPH. 1.15 is obtained by dividing 5,280 into 6,080 feet. A knot is equivalent to 6,080 feet traveled in one hour.)

Second math problem:
672 miles (24 X 28)

INTERPRETING A GRAPH (page 39)

1. merchant ship
2. caravel
3. clipper ship
4. 13

CROSSWORD PUZZLE (page 40)

FRANCISCO VASQUEZ DE CORONADO

Spain's appetite for gold was not satisfied with the conquests of Mexico and Peru. Far to the north, in what is now the southwestern part of the United States, the Seven Cities of Cibola were said to exist. These were rumored to be rich Indian cities with houses and buildings lined with turquoise and interiors filled with gold and other riches. The task of bringing this supposed new wealth under Spanish control fell to one Francisco Vasquez de Coronado.

Francisco Coronado was born in Salamanca, Spain. He came to the New World in 1535 to seek his fortune. Shortly after his arrival in Mexico he was appointed governor of New Galicia, a part of Mexico north of Mexico City. His power and prestige grew.

In 1540, Coronado was selected by the Viceroy of Mexico to lead an expedition to locate the Seven Cities of Cibola. In February of that year he rode north with 336 soldiers and several hundred Indians, as well as an ample number of horses and field guns. Based on reports that later proved to be completely false, Coronado was confident of finding Cibola.

From the start the expedition seemed destined for failure. Instead of green valleys and low hills, the conquistadors found high mountains and a wasteland with little food to eat. Still they pushed on, crossing southeast Arizona into New Mexico. At times, resistance from the Indians of the region was as much a problem as the scarcity of food.

After 77 days, Coronado came in sight of Cibola. Excitement ran high. From a distance, the Spaniards thought they were gazing at cities of gold, shining brilliantly in the sunlight. They soon discovered, however, that the golden glow they had seen was the sun illuminating the clay pueblos (houses) of the Zuni Indians who lived there. They knew then that the Seven Cities of Cibola did not exist.

Having dismissed Cibola as pure myth, Coronado moved on into Oklahoma and Kansas. He had been told by a captive Indian called "The Turk" that there was indeed a rich Indian kingdom, but that it was farther to the northeast. It was called Quivira, and gold was said to be so abundant that the king's canoes had golden oarlocks.

Coronado's search for Quivira ended in the same disappointing way as his earlier quest for Cibola. All he found on the Kansas plains was a hot sun and a group of thatched huts. Disheartened at finding no gold, he returned to Mexico a broken man. He was relieved of his position as governor of New Galicia, but remained in Mexico until his death in 1554.

Francisco Coronado never realized the importance of his undertaking. His expedition opened up the southwest to Spanish colonization. It also gathered much information about this vast region. For the first time people learned of such wonders as the Grand Canyon and the Continental Divide.

Name _____ Date _____

READING A TIME LINE

The following time line gives you important dates and events in the life of Francisco Coronado. Use it to answer the questions below.

1510	1535	1538	1540	1542	1554
Coronado born	Came to New World	Governor of New Galicia	Began search for Cibola	Exploration ends in failure	Dies in Mexico

1. How old was Coronado when he died? _____

2. How many years passed between Coronado's coming to the New World and the beginning of his search for Cibola? _____

3. How long did Coronado live after his expedition? _____

4. How long was Coronado in Mexico before he became governor of New Galicia?

   _____

5. How many years did Coronado's expedition cover? _____

ART ACTIVITIES

Choose and complete one of the following:

1. Look up and read about Cibola in an encyclopedia or history book. Then draw a picture of what the Spaniards thought the cities looked like. Color your drawing.

2. Prepare a shoebox diorama of a Zuni pueblo village.

Name _____ Date _____

A VOCABULARY EXERCISE

Select the meaning of each word as it is used in the story of Coronado. Write the letter of the correct choice on the line at the left.

_____ 1. plain: (a) easy to understand

                    (b) flat stretch of land

                    (c) common

_____ 2. divide: (a) separate into parts

                    (b) cause to disagree

                    (c) ridge of land between two regions drained by different river systems

_____ 3. wonder: (a) a strange and surprising thing

                    (b) be curious

                    (c) feeling caused by something strange and surprising

_____ 4. push (on):   (a) keep going

                    (b) go forward by force

                    (c) urge

_____ 5. broken (man):   (a) in pieces

                    (b) damaged

                    (c) weakened in spirit or strength

_____ 6. relieve: (a) make easier

                    (b) set free

                    (c) remove from a position

_____ 7. position: (a) job

                    (b) way of being placed

                    (c) place where a thing or person is

Name_____ Date _____

FRANCISCO VASQUEZ DE CORONADO CROSSWORD PUZZLE
Use the clues below and information from the narrative to complete the puzzle.

ACROSS

3. The Seven Cities of Cibola proved to be a ____ .
6. Francisco ____ .
12. Coronado also went to this state (two words).
14. It had golden oarlocks.
17. The Turk told Coronado about this place.
18. Indian tribe of Cibola.
19. The Seven Cities of_____ .
20. What a pueblo was.

DOWN

1. Indian house.
2. Coronado arrived here in 1535.
4. The mythical city's buildings were said to be lined with ____ .
5. Where Coronado was born.
7. Quivira's king had a canoe with two of these made of gold.
8. Coronado was governor of ____ ____ .
9. The ____ World.
10. Coronado came to the New World to seek his _____ .
11. The _____ Cities of Cibola.
13. A state crossed by Coronado.
15. Continental _____ .
16. Coronado never found any _____ .

FRANCISCO VASQUEZ DE CORONADO
ANSWER KEYS

READING A TIME LINE (page 43)
1. 44
2. 5 years
3. 12 years
4. 3 years
5. 2 years

A VOCABULARY EXERCISE (page 44)
1. plain: (b) flat stretch of land.
2. divide: (c) ridge of land between two regions drained by different river systems.
3. wonder: (a) a strange and surprising thing.
4. push (on): (a) keep going.
5. broken (man): (c) weakened in spirit or strength.
6. relieve: (c) remove from a position.
7. position: (a) job.

CROSSWORD PUZZLE (page 45)

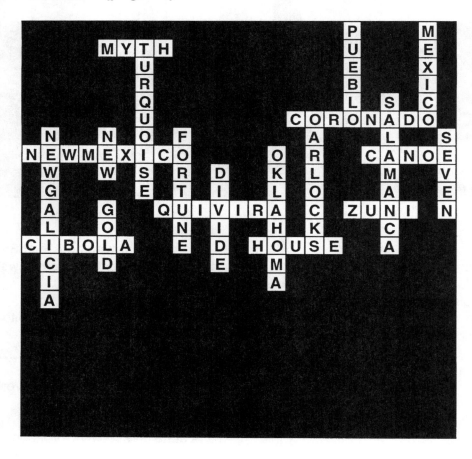

HERNANDO DE SOTO

While Coronado was unsuccessfully look-
ing for gold as far north as Kansas, another explorer was having the same bad luck to the south.

Hernando de Soto was born about 1500 in
Barcarrota, Spain. As a young man he met Pedro
Arias de Avila, the governor of Panama. Avila
quickly took a liking to young Hernando. He paid
for his education and brought him to Panama in
1519. You may recall that this was the same Pedro
Arias de Avila who had had Balboa executed for
treason in 1517.

De Soto took part in a number of explorations in the New World. He was with Pizarro in Peru
and returned to Spain with a vast fortune. This
enabled him to marry the attractive daughter of
Avila himself.

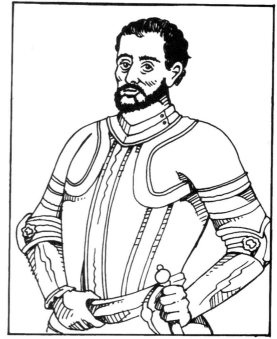

De Soto was restless living the life of a
wealthy gentleman in Spain. In 1539, using his own money, he financed an expedition to
Florida, which was described as "a land of gold." At that time, "Florida" was the name applied
to the whole southern part of the United States.

Before leaving Spain on his venture, de Soto was named governor of Cuba and
Florida by King Charles I. With 600 soldiers and 200 cavalrymen, he sailed directly to Cuba.
It was from here that he launched his exploration of Florida, landing at Tampa Bay in May
1539.

During the next four years, de Soto's search for gold took him to no less than ten
present-day southern states. He first traveled north through Georgia and Tennessee,
crossing both the Blue Ridge and Great Smoky Mountains. After finding no gold, he turned
west and pushed on. On May 21, 1541, near the site where Memphis, Tennessee, stands
today, he discovered the Mississippi River. De Soto and his company were the first white
men to cross this great body of water.

Spurred on by Indian tales of gold "farther on" (it was always farther on), de Soto
traveled through Arkansas into Oklahoma and then turned southeast into Louisiana. The
results were always the same: no gold, but hunger and hostile Indians to spare. It was while
on the Mississippi in Louisiana that de Soto took ill and died of fever on May 21, 1542. This
occurred one year to the day from when he had discovered the mighty river. His men
weighted his body with stones and buried him in the deep waters. This was done to conceal
from the Indians the fact that de Soto was not a god as they were at first led to believe.

Three hundred survivors of de Soto's expedition escaped down the Mississippi to the
Gulf of Mexico. From there they managed to cross over and take refuge in Veracruz. Once
again, Spain's quest for gold in North America proved a failure. From that point on, they
concentrated all their efforts in Central and South America.

De Soto's expedition was not all in vain, however. As with Coronado's expedition,
much information was gathered concerning the make-up and nature of a vast region of
North America.

Name _____ Date _____

CHOOSING THE CORRECT MEANING

Circle or underline the meanings of the following words as they are used in the narrative about de Soto:

1. launch:
   (a) an open motorboat

   (b) get going; start

   (c) set afloat

2. concentrate
   (a) to focus

   (b) to collect

   (c) to intensify the strength or density of

3. body:
   (a) a portion of matter

   (b) the whole physical structure of a person

   (c) group of persons or things

4. spare:
   (a) show mercy to

   (b) do without

   (c) extra

5. vain:
   (a) having too much pride in oneself

   (b) of no value

   (c) unsuccessful

6. nature:
   (a) the world

   (b) character or quality

   (c) instincts that direct behavior

Name _____ Date _____

WRITE A NEWS ARTICLE

Pretend you are a reporter covering de Soto's expedition. On your own paper write an article about the death and burial of this famous explorer.

A MAP ACTIVITY

Draw a map showing the southern part of the United States. Use a broken line to indicate the path followed by de Soto in his explorations. Use a solid line to trace the route followed earlier by Coronado. Include the names of the states each crossed in his travels.

Name _____ Date _____

HERNANDO DE SOTO CROSSWORD PUZZLE
Use the clues below and information from the narrative to complete the puzzle.

ACROSS
1. De Soto searched for this.
3. What de Soto died of.
5. _____ of Mexico.
9. Where the gold always seemed to be.
10. After de Soto's failure, the Spanish concentrated on Central and _____ America.
12. De Soto landed at Tampa _____.
13. Farthest state to the west visited by de Soto.
14. Indian civilization of Mexico.
15. Avila paid to send de Soto to _____ .
19. River discovered by de Soto.
20. _____ _____ Mountains.

DOWN
2. State where de Soto died.
4. De Soto's survivors took refuge here.
6. Name of the southern part of the United States.
7. A state visited by de Soto.
8. De Soto was governor of Florida and ___.
11. The Indians were led to believe de Soto was a ___ .
16. Pedro _____ de Avila.
17. What de Soto and Avila's daughter did.
18. Conqueror of Peru.

50

HERNANDO DE SOTO
ANSWER KEYS

CHOOSING THE CORRECT MEANING (page 48)

1. launch: (b) get going; start.
2. concentrate: (a) to focus.
3. body: (b) the whole physical structure of a person.
4. spare: (c) extra.
5. vain: (b) of no value.
6. nature: (b) character or quality.

A MAP ACTIVITY (page 49)

States listed on the map should include Arizona, New Mexico, Oklahoma, Kansas, Florida, Georgia, Tennessee, Arkansas, Louisiana, Alabama, Mississippi, South Carolina, and North Carolina.

CROSSWORD PUZZLE (page 50)

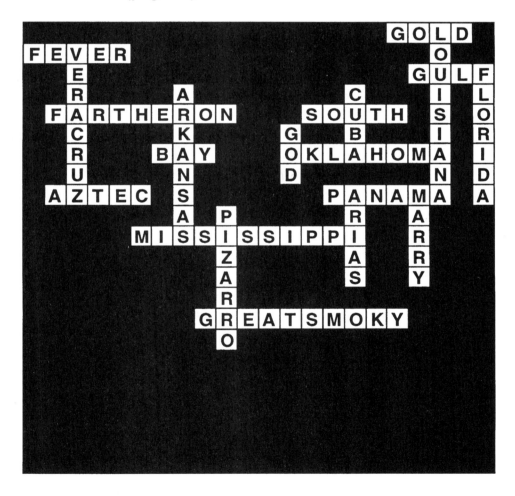

SAMUEL DE CHAMPLAIN

You will remember that Jacques Cartier discovered the St. Lawrence River in 1535 and claimed Canada for France. You may also recall that Cartier was more interested in finding gold than in establishing settlements in the New World.

The task of turning French claims into a permanent colony fell to another explorer: Samuel de Champlain. His efforts in colonization earned him the title of "Father of New France." New France was the name given to French possessions in the New World.

Samuel de Champlain was born in 1567 in the small French town of Brouage. He joined the king's service as a young man and once commanded a ship that visited Mexico City. King Henry IV was so impressed by Champlain's report of his travels that he made him royal geographer.

It was as a geographer that Champlain made his first of eleven trips to Canada. This was in March 1603. After returning home, he wrote a book entitled *The Voyages*. In the book he described his travels up the St. Lawrence River, as well as the life of the Indians with whom he came in contact.

On another trip to Canada in 1608, Champlain founded Quebec. Quebec began as a small fur-trading post and later grew into a large city. It remains today the only walled city in North America. Part of the walls surrounding the city date back to the 1600s.

In 1609 Champlain discovered a large lake that lay between what are now the states of New York and Vermont. This lake was more than 100 miles long. Today it is called Lake Champlain in his honor. Champlain came upon the lake while taking part in an Indian raiding party. He had decided to help the Algonquin and Huron Indians in their war with the Iroquois. This proved to be a mistake. In the heat of the battle, he himself shot and killed two Iroquois chiefs with his musket. The Iroquois thereafter hated the French and later sided with the Dutch and the English in their wars with the French settlers.

In 1629 the British conquered Quebec, and Champlain was taken to England as a prisoner. He remained there for several years until Canada was restored to France. Upon his return to New France he served first as lieutenant governor and then as governor. He died at Quebec on Christmas Day, 1635.

Because Champlain was more interested in settlements than in gold and silver, the French colonies in America grew and prospered. That is why he is called the "Father of New France."

Name _____ Date _____

DIVERGENT THINKING SKILLS

If you have divergent thinking skills, you possess the ability to take some important event in history and imagine what it would have been like had the result of the event turned out differently. (For example, how would the history of the United States have been altered if the South had won the Civil War?)

In the space provided, explain how the history of North America might have been different if Champlain had not become involved in the wars between the Iroquois and the Hurons/Algonquins.

_____

_____

_____

_____

_____

_____

_____

_____

_____

_____

_____

_____

_____

Name _____ Date _____

THINKING IT THROUGH

Samuel de Champlain is known in history as the "Father of New France." In the United States, George Washington is referred to as the "father" of his country. And among our Latin American neighbors, Simon Bolivar is hailed as the "George Washington of South America."

In the space provided below, write what you think it means when a nation gives the title "father" to one of its famous leaders. Point out certain things they might have done to be deserving of such an honor.

_____

_____

_____

_____

_____

_____

_____

_____

_____

LIBRARY RESEARCH

Using resources from the library prepare a two-page report on one of the following:

1. Early Quebec

2. The Great Lakes

3. The St. Lawrence River

54

Name _____ Date _____

SAMUEL DE CHAMPLAIN CROSSWORD PUZZLE

Use the clues below and information from the narrative to complete the puzzle.

ACROSS

1. Champlain made eleven _____ to America.
4. Champlain discovered a 100-mile-long ___ that was named for him.
6. Trading _____ .
8. King _____ IV of France.
14. Indian friends of the Hurons.
15. Champlain was known as the "___ of New France."
16. City founded by Champlain.
17. They and the English fought the French in America.
19. Champlain was appointed the _____ o f New France.
20. Champlain's book described his travels up this river.

DOWN

2. Enemy of the Hurons.
3. ____ -trading post.
5. Where Champlain was imprisoned.
7. Champlain's book (two words).
9. French territory in North America was called _____ France.
10. The French king made Champlain the royal _____ .
11. Champlain's first name.
12. It surrounds Quebec.
13. Indian tribe befriended by Champlain.
18. Day Champlain died (two words).

SAMUEL DE CHAMPLAIN
ANSWER KEYS

DIVERGENT THINKING SKILLS (page 53)

One possible answer: By making enemies of the Iroquois, Champlain turned them against the French. The Iroquois later sided with the British in the French and Indian War and were therefore instrumental in helping to defeat France. As a result, France lost her colonial empire in America. Students might say this could have been avoided and perhaps the situation reversed if Champlain had not sided with the Hurons and Algonquins.

THINKING IT THROUGH (page 54)

Students should point out such factors as all of the persons mentioned being instrumental in their country's birth and growth, as well as their total dedication to such causes as freedom and independence and economic well-being.

CROSSWORD PUZZLE (page 55)

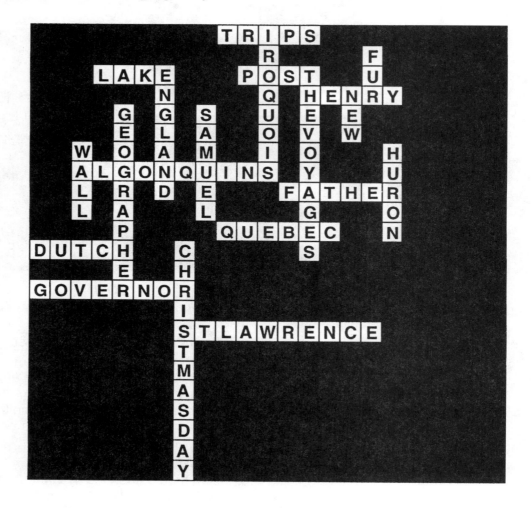

HENRY HUDSON

At the same time that Champlain was founding Quebec for France, Henry Hudson was making claims for Holland just to the south. Hudson had the unique distinction of claiming land in America for two different countries.

Henry Hudson was an Englishman who made four trips to the New World. Working first for his native England, he set sail in 1607 in his ship, the *Hopewell*, hoping to find the Northwest Passage by way of the North Pole. He failed. He made a second attempt in 1608 and failed again.

In 1609 Hudson was hired by the Dutch East India Company to again search for the Northwest Passage. He left Amsterdam, Holland, in April of that year and set sail for the northeast coast of America. After searching near Greenland for a way to the Pacific, he turned south to what is now the area of New York State.

In his ship, the *Half Moon*, Hudson sailed 140 miles up a river that we now know is 306 miles long. This river is the Hudson and is, of course, named for the explorer. Hudson sailed to a point where Albany is today. Here the Dutch would later build a fort. Because of Hudson's expedition, Holland laid claim to land in North America. In 1625 they founded New Amsterdam, which would become the city of New York after it was taken over by the English. All of the territory in America claimed by the Dutch came to be called New Netherlands.

The following year, Hudson was once again working for England. In April 1610 he set out on his fourth and last trip to the New World. Again, his goal was to find the Northwest Passage. This time he came upon a large body of water in Canada that would later be named for him. Hudson Bay was some 900 miles long and 500 miles wide. Because of this discovery, England claimed the rich lands around the bay.

Henry Hudson was convinced that he had found the way to the Pacific. But after traveling south in his ship, the *Discovery*, the water turned to ice. The *Discovery* was icebound in James Bay, as the southern part of Hudson Bay is called. Hudson and his crew were forced to spend a terrible winter trapped on the ice. His young son was also among those stranded.

In June 1611 the ice melted, and Hudson planned to continue his search for the Pacific. But his crew, desiring to return to Europe, mutinied and took over the ship. What followed is one of the most shameful incidents in English history. Hudson, his son, and seven loyal and sick crewmen were put adrift in a small boat. They were given no food, water, or weapons. They were never heard from again.

Name _____ Date _____

SEQUENCING

Put the following events in order by writing the numbers 1 to 5 on the lines to the left.

_____ Hudson sails in the *Hopewell.*

_____ The *Half Moon* sails up the Hudson River.

_____ The Dutch establish New Amsterdam.

_____ The *Discovery* sails into Hudson Bay.

_____ Hudson is put adrift by a mutinous crew.

A MATH ACTIVITY

Assume that Hudson's *Discovery* traveled at a top speed of 3.5 knots, or approximately 4 miles per hour. Under ideal weather conditions, how long (in days) would it have taken the ship to travel the length of Hudson Bay, a distance of 900 miles? _____

WRITE AN EYEWITNESS ACCOUNT

Pretend you are a member of the crew of the *Discovery* that put Henry Hudson, his son, and seven loyal crewmen adrift in Hudson Bay. On the lines below and on the back of this page write an eyewitness account of the scene, describing the emotions and actions of both the mutineers and those who were abandoned.

_____

_____

_____

_____

_____

Name _____ Date _____

AN ART ACTIVITY

Find in an encyclopedia or history book a drawing of either the *Hopewell*, the *Half Moon*, or the *Discovery*. In the space provided, draw a sketch of one of these ships.

Name _____ Date _____

HENRY HUDSON CROSSWORD PUZZLE

Use the clues below and information from the narrative to complete the puzzle.

ACROSS

2. The Hudson _____ is 306 miles long.
3. _____ East India Company.
4. One of Hudson's ships.
6. What Hudson was searching for.
9. The Dutch built a fort here.
10. Green _____.
14. Crime committed by Hudson's crew.
15. Early name of New York City.
19. Name given to Dutch lands in America.

DOWN

1. Hudson's last ship.
4. One of Hudson's ships (two words).
5. Henry _____.
7. Country of the Dutch East India Company.
8. Dutch _____ Indies.
11. Hudson's crew wanted to return here.
12. Hudson made four trips to the _____ World.
13. A large body of water in Canada discovered by Hudson was named Hudson _____.
16. Number of crewmen loyal to Hudson.
17. Hudson was put _____ in a small boat.
18. What sails need to work.

HENRY HUDSON
ANSWER KEYS

SEQUENCING (page 58)
1, 2, 5, 3, 4

A MATH ACTIVITY (page 58)
Approximately $9\frac{1}{3}$ days.

(900 miles divided by 4 MPH = 225.
225 divided by 24 hours = 9.375.)

CROSSWORD PUZZLE (page 60)

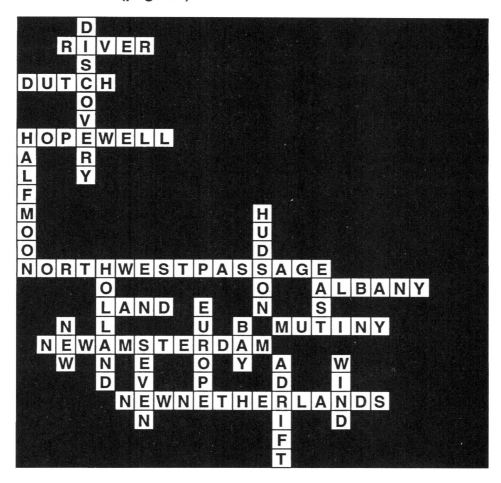

BIBLIOGRAPHY

The following books proved helpful in writing *Explorers of the New World:*

Hale, John R. and the editors of Time-Life Books. *The Age of Exploration* (from The Great Ages of Man). New York: Time Incorporated, 1966.

Horgan, Paul. *Conquistadors in North American History.* New York: Farrar, Straus, and Company, 1963.

Johnson, Thomas H. *The Oxford Companion to American History.* New York: Oxford University Press, 1966.

Morrison, Samuel Eliot. *The Oxford History of the American People.* New York: Oxford University Press, 1965.

Protter, Eric. *Explorers and Explorations.* New York: Grosset & Dunlap, 1962.

Stirling, Mathew W. *Indians of the Americas.* Washington, D.C.: The National Geographic Society, 1955.